SPORTS FOR SPROUTS

GYMNASTICS

Holly Karapetkova

ROURKE PUBLISHING

Vero Beach, Florida 32964

www.rourkepublishing.com

Photo credits: All photography by Renee Brady for Blue Door Publishing, except Cover © Wendy Nero; Title Page © Wendy Nero, Crystal Kirk, Leah-Anne Thompson, vnosokin, Gerville Hall, Rob Marmion; Page 8 © © Vyacheslav Osokin; Page 12 © Robert J. Daveant; Page 14 © Tony Wear; Sidebar Silhouettes © Sarah Nicholl

Editor: Meg Greve

Cover and page design by Nicola Stratford, Blue Door Publishing

Acknowledgements: Thank you to *Tumbleweeds* (www.tumbleweedsgym.net), Melbourne, Florida, for their assistance on this project

Library of Congress Cataloging-in-Publication Data

Karapetkova, Holly.
  Gymnastics / Holly Karapetkova.
     p. cm. -- (Sports for sprouts)
  ISBN 978-1-60694-325-0 (hard cover)
  ISBN 978-1-60694-825-5 (soft cover)
  ISBN 978-1-60694-566-7 (bilingual)
  1. Gymnastics--Juvenile literature. I. Title.
GV461.3.K37 2010
796.44--dc22

                                    2009002258

Rourke Publishing
Printed in the United States of America, North Mankato, Minnesota
03022011
030111LP-A

www.rourkepublishing.com - rourke@rourkepublishing.com
Post Office Box 643328 Vero Beach, Florida 32964

I am a gymnast.

3

4

At my gymnastics class, I wear a **leotard**.

We stretch our arms and legs.

We tumble on
the mats.

We do **somersaults.**

11

We walk on the balance beam. Don't fall!

We flip around
the bars.

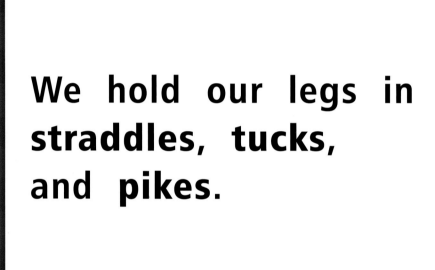

We hold our legs in **straddles, tucks,** and **pikes.**

It's fun to use the **mini trampoline** to jump high.

We cheer for each other.
We always try our best!

21

Glossary

leotard (LEE-uh-tard): A leotard is a tight piece of clothing that covers the body from the shoulders to the thighs. Dancers and gymnasts wear leotards.

mini trampoline (MIN-ee tram-puh-LEEN): A mini trampoline is a piece of exercise equipment made of strong canvas attached to a frame with springs. It allows gymnasts to bounce up high.

pikes (PIKES): In a pike, the gymnast keeps the legs straight.

somersaults (SUHM-ur-sawlts): Somersaults are rolls where the head goes down on the ground and the body turns over the head. Another word for somersaults is forward rolls.

straddles (STRAD-uhlz): In a straddle, the gymnast's legs spread wide out to either side.

tucks (TUHKS): In a tuck, the gymnast's knees are bent and the legs are pulled in close to the chest.

Index

Websites

www.usa-gymnastics.org

www.fig-gymnastics.com

www.gymnasticszone.com

About The Author

Holly Karapetkova, Ph.D., loves writing books and poems for kids and adults. She teaches at Marymount University and lives in the Washington, D.C., area with her husband, her son K.J., and her two dogs, Muffy and Attila.